A Sampling of Tradition

The precursor to today's cross stitch, needlework samplers are an essential — and enchanting — thread in the heritage of modern stitchery. Early samplers were created as reference tools for stitches and designs, since women had no pattern books. By the mid-1800s, samplers had taken on their most recognized form: *the "schoolgirl" sampler.* A staple of a young girl's education, these samplers featured decorative borders, alphabets, religious verses, and motifs, often houses, flowers, and animals. I... age, pictorial samplers became more ... for their detailed illustrations, these sam... types of stitches until it was common to use o... one stitch — the cross stitch.

Whether you're a history buff or just enjoy the strong designs and simple appeal of samplers, you're sure to treasure these modern-day tributes to the classic sampler. We've carefully chosen eight exquisite designs from a selection of samplers published in the much-adored magazine, *For The Love Of Cross Stitch*. From samplers designed to honor special family members to gentle reminders of our daily blessings, these nostalgic works of art will be cherished for years to come.

Leisure Arts, Inc.
Maumelle, Arkansas

Table of Contents

Seasonal Band Sampler

Colorful blooms and jubilant angels celebrate earth's renewal in this cheerful, homey sampler. The framed piece and coordinating projects emulate the radiance of springtime with accessories for the bedroom, bath, and kitchen.

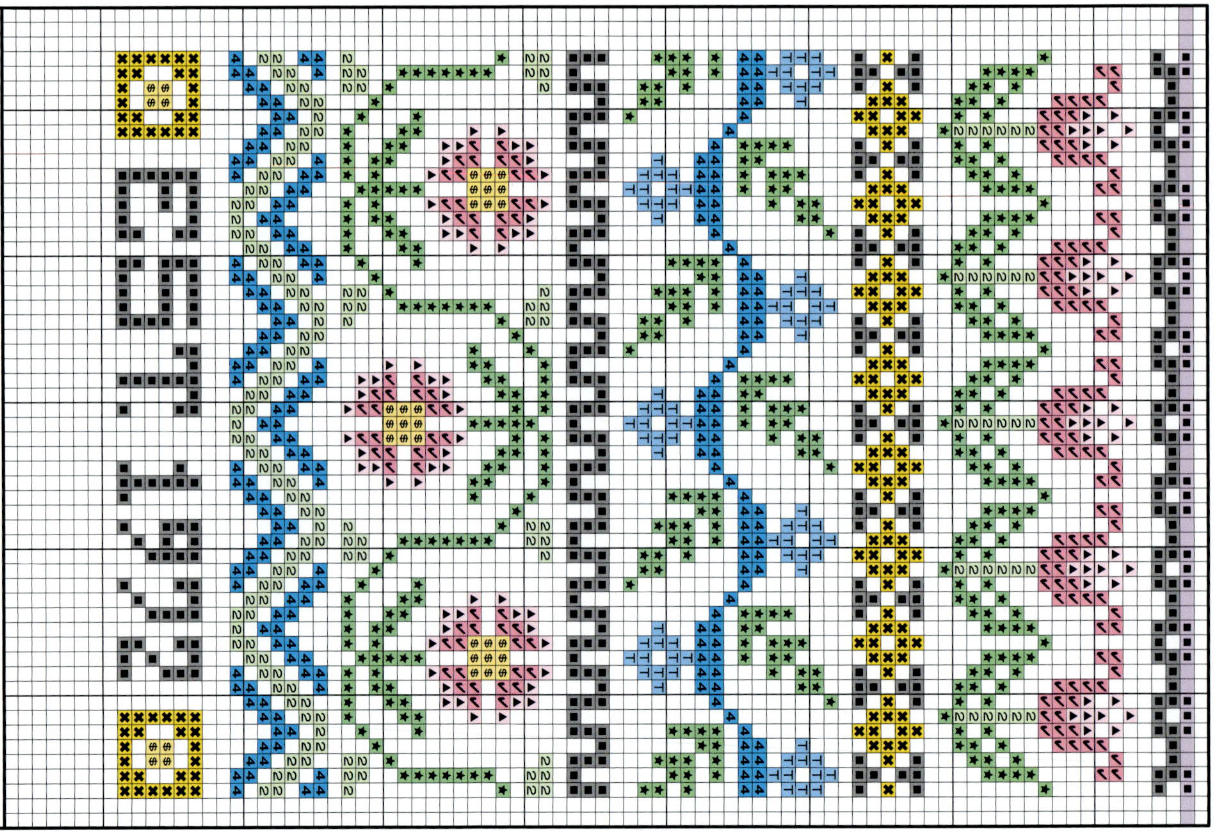

X	DMC	ANC.	COLOR
	309	42	dk pink
	310	403	black
	415	398	grey
	472	253	lt green
	743	302	yellow
	754	1012	flesh
	783	307	dk yellow
	799	136	dk blue
	840	379	brown
	899	52	pink
	913	204	green
	3761	928	blue

Purple area indicates last row of top section of design.

Note: Projects shown on pages 3, 5, and above. All projects were stitched using 3 strands of floss for Cross Stitch.

Framed Piece: The entire design was stitched on a 12" x 20" piece of Antique White Aida (14 ct). It was custom framed. Personalize year with numerals provided.

Mug: A portion of the design was stitched on a 10 1/4" x 3 1/2" Parchment Vinyl Weave™ (14 ct) mug insert. It was inserted in a White Mugs Your Way™ mug. Hand wash mug to protect stitchery.

Towels: Portions of the design were stitched on the White 14 ct insert of White Fingertip towels. Starting in the center, repeat the design as desired to each edge of towel.

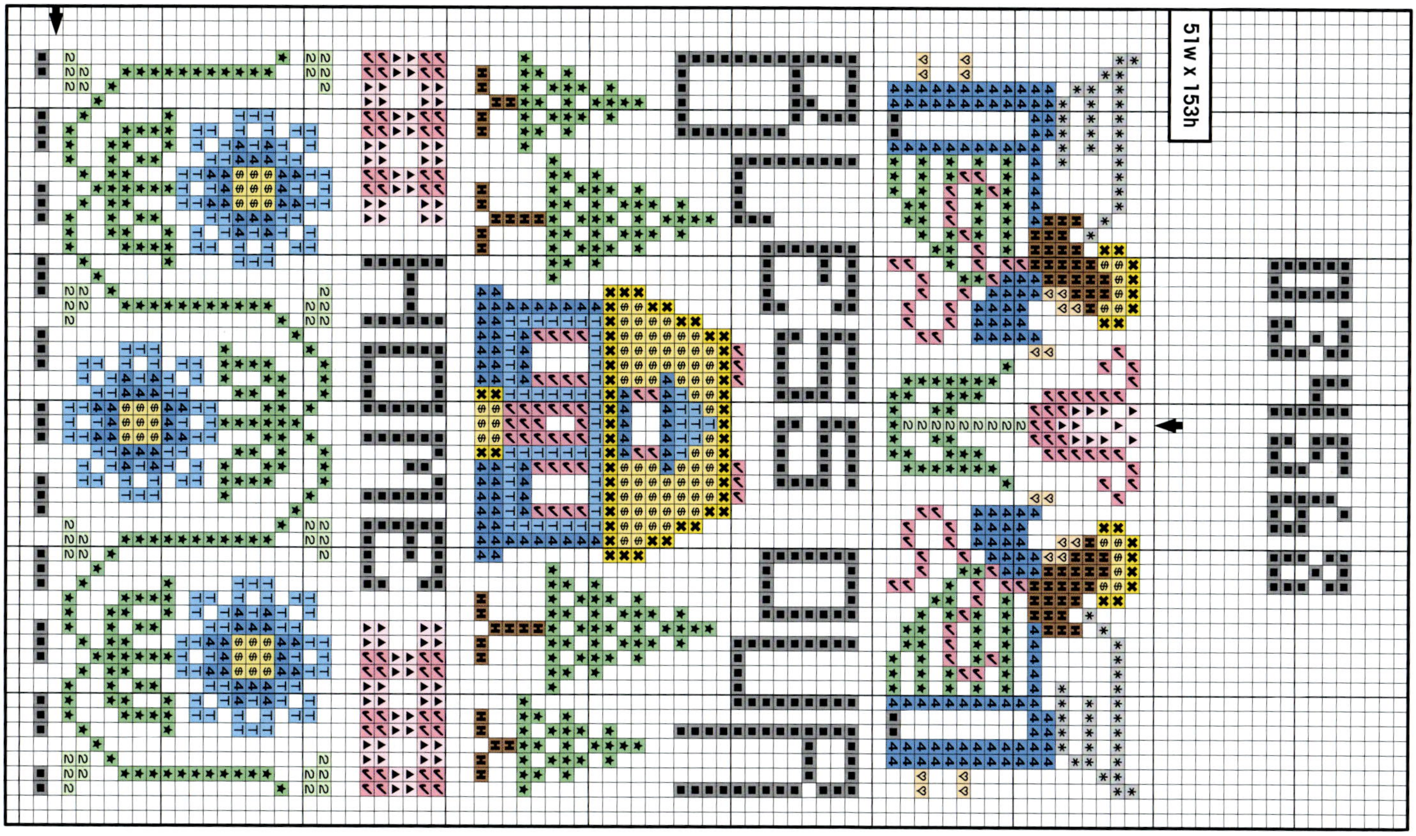

Bread Cloth: A portion of the design was stitched on one side of a White Royal Classic Breadcover (14 ct) 7 squares from beginning of fringe. To finish corners, cut 2" squares out of each corner. Machine stitch 1/2" away from raw edge; fringe fabric to machine-stitched lines.

Door Pillow: The top portion of the design was stitched on a 12" square of Antique White Aida (14 ct). It was made into a pillow. See Bless Our Home Pillow Finishing, page 28.

Design by Deborah Lambein.

My Mother, My Friend

Honor your mother in a loving way with an ensemble that's rich in endearing qualities. The thoughtful sampler, given with a quick-to-stitch sachet, porcelain jar, candle band, and towel, will provide beautiful mementos to touch a Mom's heart.

Note: Projects shown on page 6. All projects were stitched using 2 strands of floss for Cross Stitch and 1 for Backstitch. Refer to chart for type of thread and number of strands used for Specialty Stitches. See Specialty Stitch Diagrams, pages 27 and 28.

Framed Piece: The entire design was stitched on a 14" x 19" piece of Zweigart® Cream Belfast Linen (32 ct). It was stitched over 2 fabric threads. Personalize and date design using DMC 3782 floss and alphabet and numerals from chart. It was custom framed.

Candle Band: A portion of the design (refer to photo on page 6) was stitched on a 5" x 13" piece of Zweigart® Cream Cashel Linen® (28 ct). It was stitched over 2 fabric threads.

For candle band, you will need an 11" length of 2¼"w satin ribbon and clear-drying craft glue.

Centering design, trim stitched piece to measure 2½" x 11".

Turn long edges of stitched piece ½" to wrong side; press. Referring to photo, center wrong side of stitched piece on satin ribbon; glue in place.

Wrap candle band around candle, turning raw edges to wrong side so that ends meet; blind stitch short edges together.

Sachet Bag: A portion of the design (refer to photo on page 6) was stitched on an 11" x 9½" piece of Zweigart® Antique White Aida (14 ct).

For sachet bag, you will need an 8" length of ⅞" w flat lace, 22" length of ¼"w ribbon, polyester fiberfill, and scented oil.

Note: Use ½" seam allowance for all seams.

Centering design horizontally and allowing a 4" margin at top of design and a 1" margin at bottom of design, trim stitched piece to measure 8$^{1}/_{2}$" x 6". Matching right sides and short edges, sew bag together; press seam open. With seam at center back, sew across bottom of bag. Trim seam allowances diagonally at corners; turn sachet bag right side out, carefully pushing corners outward. Turn top edge $^{1}/_{4}$" to wrong side and press; turn $^{1}/_{4}$" to wrong side again and hem. Press short edges of lace $^{1}/_{2}$" to wrong side. Blind stitch straight edge of lace to wrong side of top edge of bag; turn bag right side out and stuff with polyester fiberfill. Place a few drops of scented oil on a small amount of fiberfill and insert in bag. Tie ribbon in a bow around bag; trim ends as desired.

Porcelain Jar: Portions of the design (refer to photo on page 6) were stitched on an 8" square of Zweigart® Cream Cashel Linen® (28 ct). They were stitched over 2 fabric threads allowing 4 rows between "MOM" and the border designs. It was inserted in the lid of a round porcelain jar (3$^{1}/_{2}$" dia. opening). **Towel:** A portion of the design (refer to photo on page 6) was stitched on the 14 ct insert of a Charles Craft, Inc.® Ecru E-Z Stitch Towel.

Design by Linda Culp Calhoun.

STITCH COUNT (102w x 181h)	
14 count	7$^{3}/_{8}$" x 13"
16 count	6$^{3}/_{8}$" x 11$^{3}/_{8}$"
18 count	5$^{3}/_{4}$" x 10$^{1}/_{8}$"
22 count	4$^{3}/_{4}$" x 8$^{1}/_{4}$"

Proverbs 7:4 Sampler

As the verse on this nostalgic sampler illustrates, sisters share a special bond. Honor the woman you often turn to for wisdom and understanding with a sentimental display of devotion. Overdyed floss lends old-fashioned charm to the framed piece. For your convenience, we've also included an alternate color key for regular DMC floss, which was used on the bookmark and decorative box.

X	SAMPLER THREAD	DMC	B'ST	COLOR
8	Adobe	758		flesh
✦	Avocado	3364		green
■	Black Crow	310	/	black
✓	Brandy	434		brown
●	Cinnamon	801	/	dk brown
M	Cornflower	931	/	blue
♥	Cranberry	814		burgundy
✕	Dried Thyme	936		dk green
★	Gold Leaf	3821		yellow
H	Midnight	3750		dk blue
•	Oatmeal	ecru	/	ecru

X	SAMPLER THREAD	DMC	COLOR
5	Old Brick	3712	salmon
●	Cranberry	814	burgundy French Knot

Grey area indicates last row of top section of design.

SAMPLER THREAD	DMC	SPECIALTY STITCH
Avocado	3364	Satin Stitch
Cinnamon	801	Algerian Eye Stitch
Cranberry	814	Four-sided Stitch
Midnight	3750	Stem Stitch

STITCH COUNT (136w x 184h)			
14 count	9 3/4"	x	13 1/4"
16 count	8 1/2"	x	11 1/2"
18 count	7 5/8"	x	10 1/4"
22 count	6 1/4"	x	8 3/8"

Note: Projects shown on page 9. All projects were stitched over 2 fabric threads using 2 strands of floss or Sampler Threads for Cross Stitch, Backstitch, French Knots, and Specialty Stitches. See Specialty Stitch Diagrams, pages 28 and 29.

Framed Piece: The entire design was stitched on an 18" x 21" piece of Wichelt Imports, Inc. Chestnut Linen (32 ct) using Sampler Threads by The Gentle Art. Refer to color key to stitch using DMC floss colors. It was custom framed.

Box: A portion of the design (refer to photo) was stitched on a 15" x 13" piece of Wichelt Imports, Inc. Chestnut Linen (32 ct). It was inserted in the lid of a purchased box (7" x 5" opening).

Bookmark: A portion of the design (refer to photo) was stitched on an 8" x 13" piece of Wichelt Imports, Inc. Chestnut Linen (32 ct). It was made into a bookmark.

For bookmark, center design and trim stitched piece to measure 4" x 9 1/4". Machine stitch 1/4" away from edge of design on short edges. Fringe to machine-stitched line. For remaining edges, turn fabric 1/4" to wrong side and press; turn 1/4" to wrong side again and hem.

Design by Susan Stadler.

Say unto wisdom,
Thou art my sister;
and call understanding
thy kinswoman. Prov. 7:4
ABCDEFGHIJKLMNOP

Noah's Sampler

The beloved story of Noah and his Ark inspires young and old alike. Depicting images from that faithful passage, this charming sampler can be personalized with the stitcher's initials and custom framed to accent any decor. For two quick coordinating projects, the olive tree and ark motifs are stitched on coasters. What thoughtful gift ideas!

#1(109w x 87h)

X	DMC	B'ST	ANC.	COLOR
♥	315		1019	mauve
■	844	/	1041	charcoal
★	931		1034	blue
+	3362		263	green
✓	3790		393	khaki
	Grey area indicates last row of left section of design.			

Projects shown on page 12.

Design #1: The design was stitched on a 16" x 14" piece of Platinum Cashel Linen® (28 ct). It was stitched over 2 fabric threads. Three strands of floss were used for Cross Stitch and 1 for Backstitch.

Designs #2 & #3: Each design was stitched on a 6" square of Platinum Cashel Linen® (28 ct). They were stitched over 2 fabric threads. Three strands of floss were used for Cross Stitch and 1 for Backstitch. They were made into coasters.

For each coaster, trim stitched piece 1" larger than design on all sides. Cut a piece of felt slightly larger than stitched piece for backing. Matching wrong sides, machine stitch stitched piece and felt together 1/2" away from edge of design. Fringe fabric to within one thread of machine stitching. Cut a 1/2" square from each corner.

Designs by Kandace Thomas.

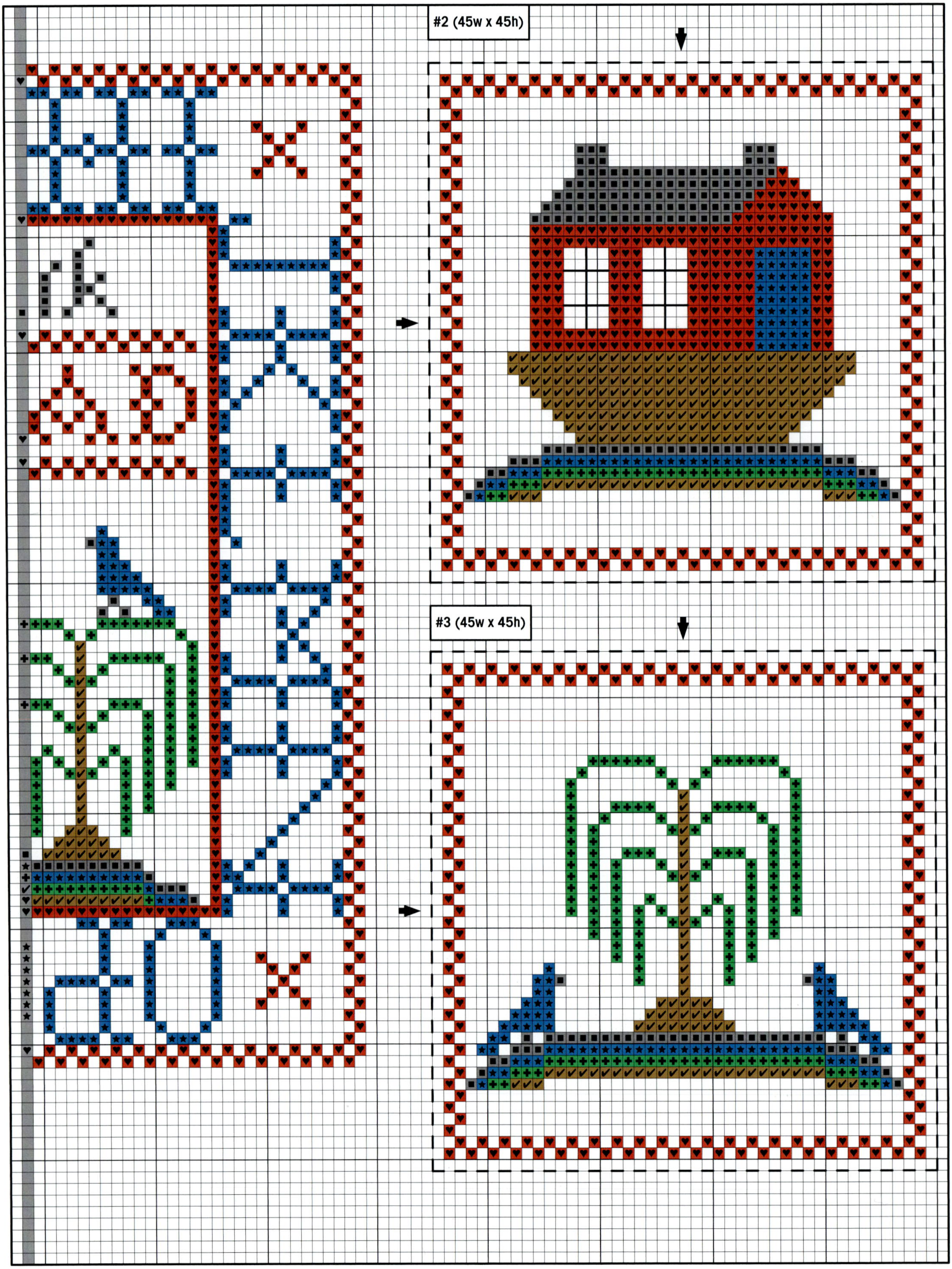
#2 (45w x 45h)
#3 (45w x 45h)

Heirloom Sampler

For the stitcher who loves to marvel at antique works, this charming sampler encompasses a legacy. The classic design features many of the most popular images found in authentic samplers, including the name of a fictitious stitcher for added credibility!

X	DMC	ANC.	COLOR
△	223	895	pink
■	310	403	black
Π	400	351	rust
❖	500	683	dk green
Σ	501	878	green
%	502	877	lt green
$	676	891	gold
P	754	1012	peach
♥	815	43	red
★	823	152	dk blue
●	838	380	dk brown
✔	839	360	brown
2	841	378	dk beige
✚	920	1004	orange
♡	931	1034	blue
•	991	189	blue green
*	3033	391	beige

Grey area indicates last row of top section of design.

STITCH COUNT (141w x 163h)			
14 count	10 1/8"	x	11 3/4"
16 count	8 7/8"	x	10 1/4"
18 count	7 7/8"	x	9 1/8"
22 count	6 1/2"	x	7 1/2"

The design (shown on page 15) was stitched on a 19" x 21" piece of Charles Craft, Inc.® Natural Irish Linen (26 ct). It was stitched over 2 fabric threads. Three strands of floss were used for Cross Stitch. It was custom framed.

Grateful Heart Sampler

Warm colors and simple imagery come together in our lovely alphabet sampler. The time-honored house illustration symbolizes the warmth that family members bring to life, while the gingham heart and lovely flowers represent the importance of a fresh perspective of hope and thanksgiving.

X	DMC	ANC.	COLOR
	435	1046	dk tan
	436	1045	tan
	437	362	lt tan
	676	891	lt gold
	712	926	cream
	780	310	dk gold
	869	944	brown
	918	341	copper
	3051	681	dk green
	3052	262	green
	3053	261	lt green
	3787		grey
	3802	1019	dk mauve

Grey area indicates last row of top section of design.

Note: Project shown on page 18.
The design (shown on page 18) was stitched on a 15" x 17" piece of Zweigart® Antique White Aida (14 ct). Two strands of floss were used for Cross Stitch. It was custom framed.

Framed Piece: The entire design was stitched on a 15" x 17" piece of Zweigart® Antique White Aida (14 ct). It was custom framed.

Design by Diane Williams.

STITCH COUNT (99w x 130h)	
14 count	7 1/8" x 9 3/8"
16 count	6 1/4" x 8 1/8"
18 count	5 1/2" x 7 1/4"
22 count	4 1/2" x 6"

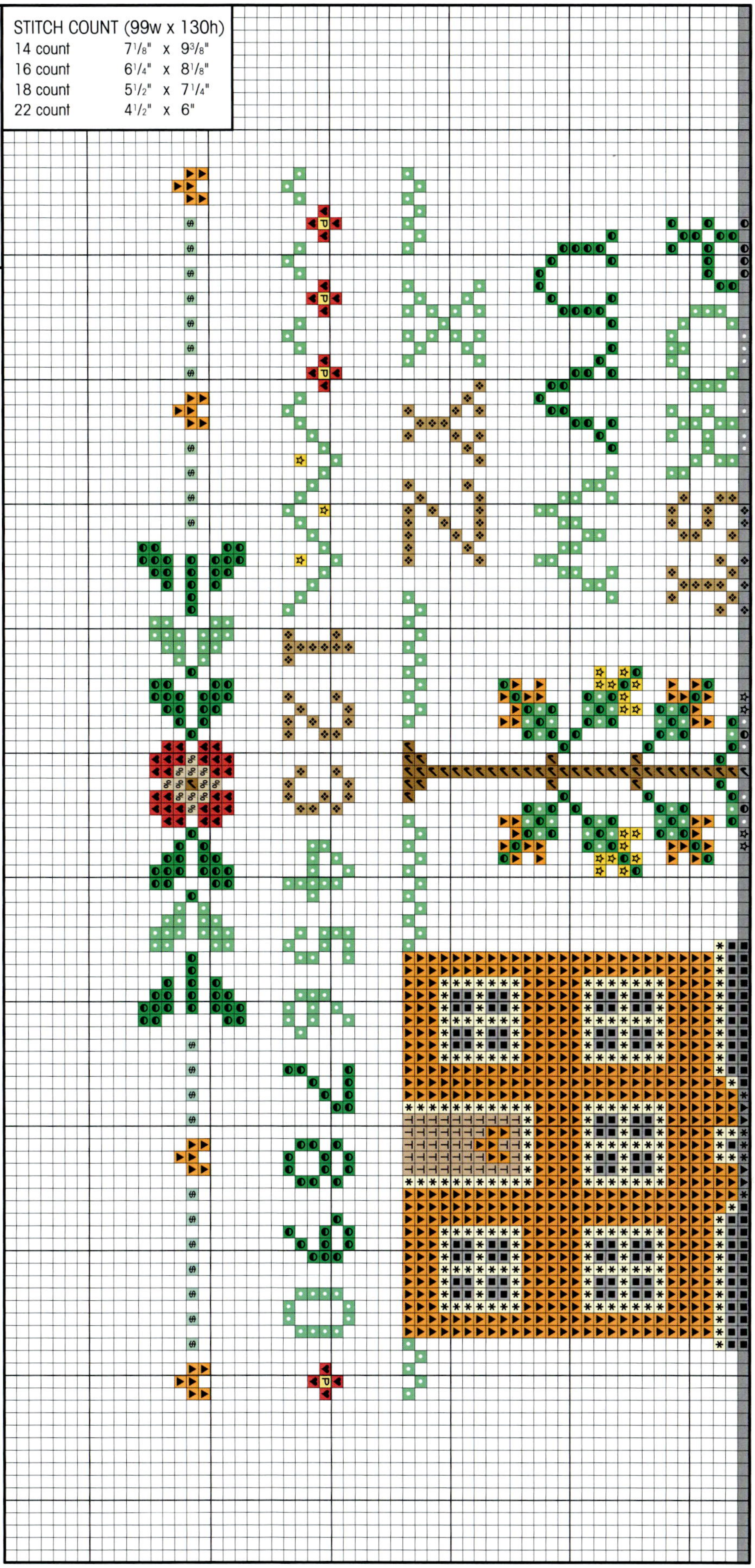

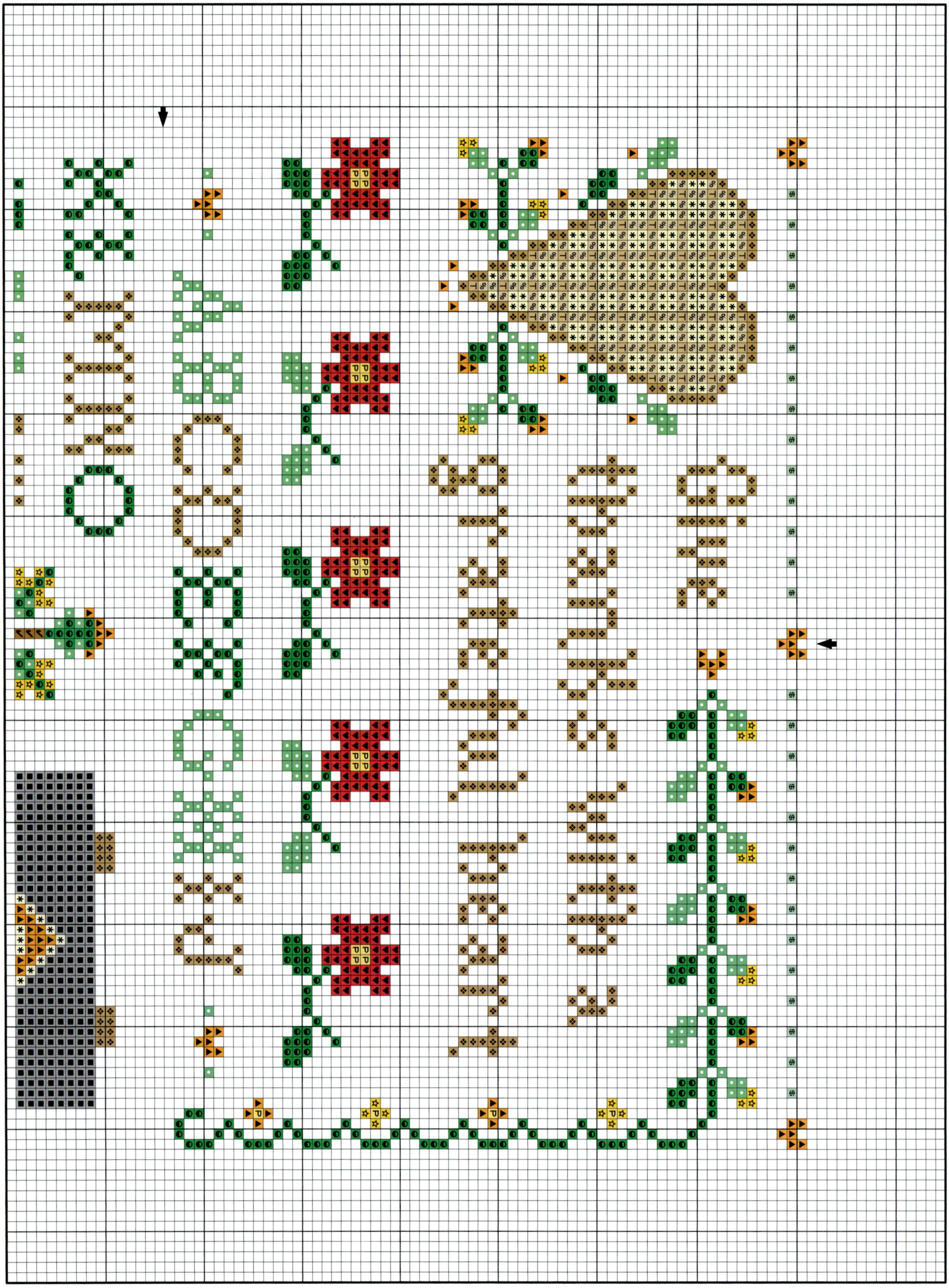

Life and *Love Sampler*

This beautiful sampling of stitchery shares an uplifting reminder of the simple goodness of life and love. Starry satin stitches and pretty floral motifs illustrate these principles for daily living. What a timeless wedding or anniversary surprise.

FRIENDSHIPS WE SHARE GROW STRONGER WITH TIME
LOVE IS A FLOWER THAT BLOOMS
WITH EVERY SEASON OF THE HEART
STAR OF LIGHT
CROWN OF LIFE
ANCHOR OF HOPE
KEY TO HEAVEN
RINGS OF FAITH
HEARTS OF LOVE

X	DMC	ANC.	COLOR	X	DMC	B'ST	ANC.	COLOR
=	ecru	387	ecru	◉	758		882	peach
C	224	893	pink	×	924	/	851	blue
+	315	1019	mauve	☆	948		1011	lt peach
★	501	878	dk green	■	3041		871	purple
□	503	876	green	|||	ecru Satin Stitch			
V	504	1042	lt green	■	Grey area indicates last row of top section of design.			
◇	644	830	beige					
8	676	891	yellow					

STITCH COUNT (81w x 219h)

14 count	$5^{7}/_{8}$"	x	$15^{3}/_{4}$"
16 count	$5^{1}/_{8}$"	x	$13^{3}/_{4}$"
18 count	$4^{1}/_{2}$"	x	$12^{1}/_{4}$"
22 count	$3^{3}/_{4}$"	x	10"

The design (shown on page 21) was stitched on a 14" x 24" piece of Light Mocha Cashel Linen® (28 ct). It was stitched over 2 fabric threads. Three strands of floss were used for Satin Stitch, 2 for Cross Stitch, and 1 for Backstitch. To personalize sampler, use alphabet and numerals provided in chart and DMC #315 . It was custom framed.

Design by Dixie Barker Shoemaker.

Harvest Band Sampler

Times of peace and plenty have always presented a bounty of reasons to rejoice. The detailed style and nostalgic appearance of this traditional harvest sampler form an extraordinary piece of workmanship that will remind each of us to enjoy our blessings.

STITCH COUNT (81w x 170h)			
14 count	5 7/8"	x	12 1/4"
16 count	5 1/8"	x	10 5/8"
18 count	4 1/2"	x	9 1/2"
22 count	3 3/4"	x	7 3/4"

X	DMC	B'ST	ANC.	COLOR
★	312		979	blue
✓	327		100	purple
♥	347		1025	red
Σ	433		358	brown
⊖	562	⁄	210	dk green
*	781		309	gold
8	922		1003	orange
H	989		242	green
▢	Grey area indicates first row of bottom section of design.			

All projects were stitched using 2 strands of floss for Cross Stitch and 1 for Backstitch.

The design (shown on page 24) was stitched on a 14" x 20" piece of Light Mocha Cashel Linen® (28 ct). It was stitched over 2 fabric threads. Two strands of floss were used for Cross Stitch and 1 for Backstitch. Personalize and date design using DMC 989 floss and alphabet and numerals from chart. It was custom framed.

Design by Deborah Lambein.

GENERAL INSTRUCTIONS

WORKING WITH CHARTS

How to Read Charts: Each of the designs is shown in chart form. Each colored square on the chart represents one Cross Stitch. Colored dots represent French Knots. The straight lines on the chart indicate Backstitch.

Each chart is accompanied by a color key. This key indicates the color of floss to use for each stitch on the chart. The headings on the color key are for Cross Stitch (**X**), DMC color number (**DMC**), Backstitch (**B'ST**), Anchor color number (**ANC**), and color name (**COLOR**). Color key columns should be read vertically and horizontally to determine type of stitch and floss color.

How to Determine Finished Size: The finished size of your design will depend on the thread count per inch of the fabric being used. To determine the finished size of the design on different fabrics, divide the number of squares (stitches) in the width of the charted design by the thread count of the fabric. For example, a charted design with a width of 80 squares worked on 14 count Aida will yield a design $5^3/_4$" wide. Repeat for the number of squares (stitches) in the height of the charted design. (**Note:** To work over two fabric threads, divide the number of squares by one-half the thread count.) Then add the amount of background you want plus a generous amount for finishing.

Where to Start: The horizontal and vertical centers of the charted design are shown by arrows. You may start at any point on the charted design, but be sure the design will be centered on the fabric. Locate the center of fabric by folding in half, top to bottom and again left to right. On the charted design, count the number of squares from the center of the chart to the determined starting point; then from the fabric's center, count out the same number of fabric threads.

STITCH DIAGRAMS

Counted Cross Stitch (X): Work a Cross Stitch to correspond to each colored square on the chart. For horizontal rows, work stitches in two journeys (**Fig. 1**). For vertical rows, complete each stitch as shown (**Fig. 2**). When working over two fabric threads, work Cross Stitch as shown in **Fig. 3**. When the chart shows a Backstitch crossing a colored square (**Fig. 4**), a Cross Stitch should be worked first; then the Backstitch (**Fig. 5**) should be worked on top of the Cross Stitch.

Fig. 1

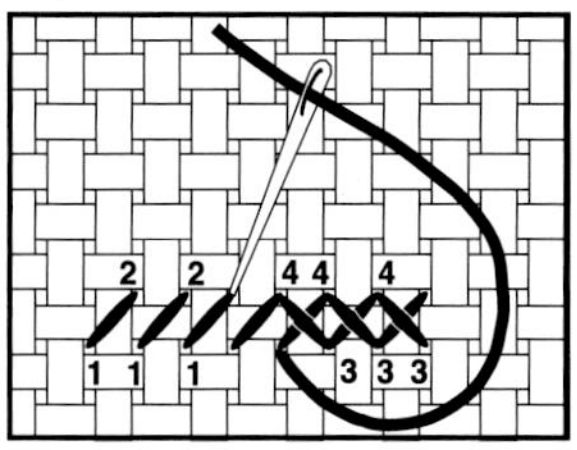

Fig. 2

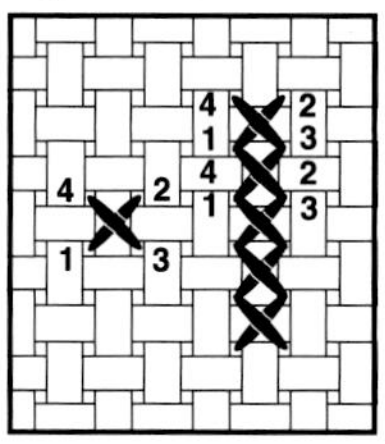

Fig. 3

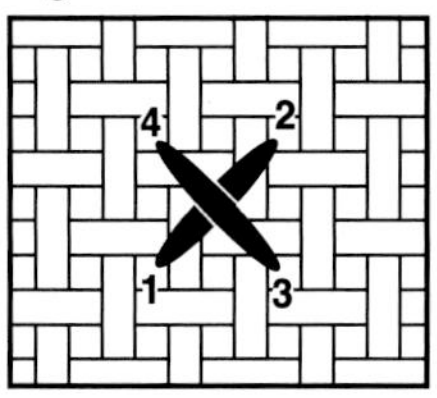

Fig. 4

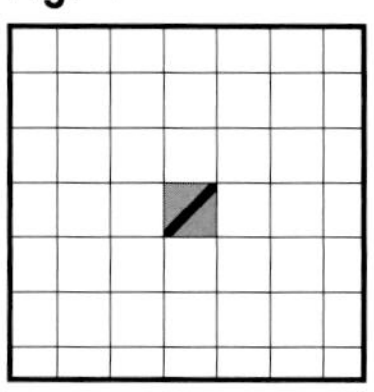

Backstitch (B'ST): For outline detail, Backstitch (shown on chart and on color key by black or colored straight lines) should be worked after the design has been completed (**Fig. 5**).

Fig. 5

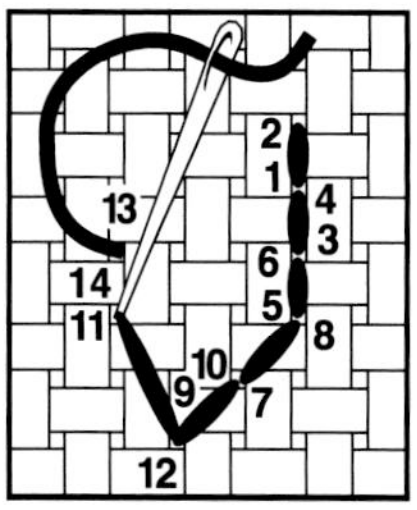

French Knot: Bring needle up at 1. Wrap floss once around needle and insert needle at 2, holding end of floss with non-stitching fingers (**Fig. 6**). Tighten knot; then pull needle through fabric, holding floss until it must be released. For larger knot, use more strands; wrap only once.

Fig. 6

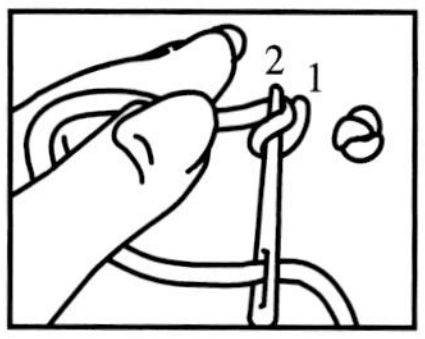

SPECIALTY STITCH DIAGRAMS

Note: Bring threaded needle up at 1 and all odd numbers and down at 2 and all even numbers.

Algerian Eye Stitch: An "eye" is formed in the center of this stitch. Come up at 1, go down in center, and pull tightly toward 3. Come up at 3, go down in center, and pull tightly toward 5; continue working in this manner until stitch is complete (stitches 5-15) (**Fig. 7**). Work row of Algerian Eye Stitches from right to left.

Fig. 7

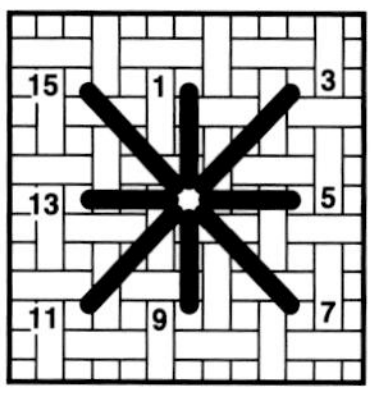

Double Cross Stitch: This decorative stitch is worked as a continuous stitch. Work large Cross Stitch (stitches 1-4) first, then work Upright Cross (stitches 5-8) over center of large Cross Stitch as shown in **Fig 8**. The top stitch of the Upright Cross must be made in the same direction on all Double Cross Stitches worked.

Fig. 8

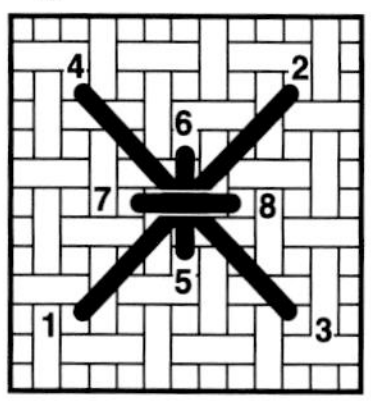

Four-sided Stitch: This continuous stitch is worked from left to right. Come up at 1 and pull tightly toward 2; then go down at 2 and pull tightly toward 1. Work stitches 3-14 in same manner (**Fig. 9**). Continue working in the same manner to end of row.

Fig. 9

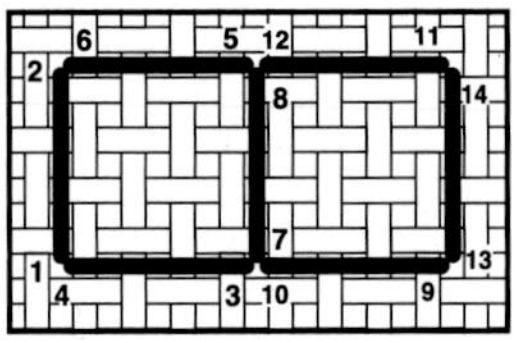

Long Arm Cross Stitch: This overlapping stitch is worked continuously from left to right. Complete first stitch (stitches 1-4); then work next stitch (stitches 5-8) as shown in **Fig. 10**. Work all consecutive stitches in the same manner as stitches 5-8.

Fig. 10

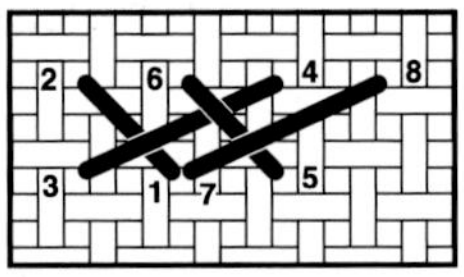

Pins Stitch: This stitch is a series of straight stitches worked side by side (**Fig. 11**). Complete stitch 1-2, come up at 3, and pull tightly; go down at 4, come up at 5, and pull tightly. Continue working in the same manner to end of row.

Fig. 11

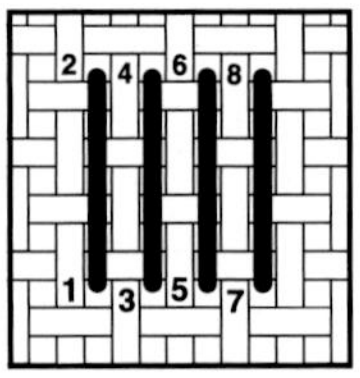

Queen Stitch: This decorative stitch forms a diamond shape. Work a long stitch (stitch 1-2) loosely and catch with a short stitch (stitch 3-4) (**Fig. 12**). Complete stitch (stitches 5-16), catching each long stitch with a short stitch as shown in **Figs. 13-14**.

Fig. 12

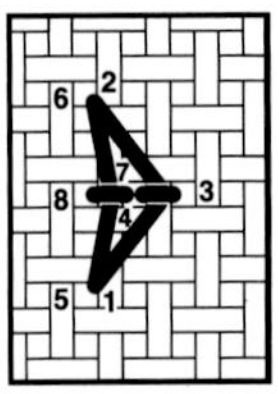

Fig. 13

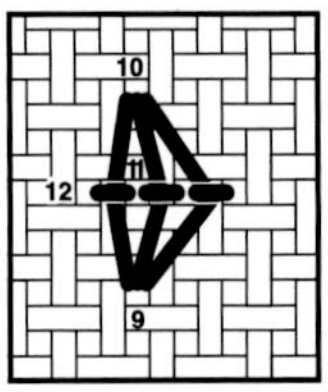

Fig. 14

Satin Stitch: This stitch is a series of straight stitches worked side by side (**Fig. 15**). The number of threads worked over and the direction of stitches will vary according to the chart.

Fig. 15

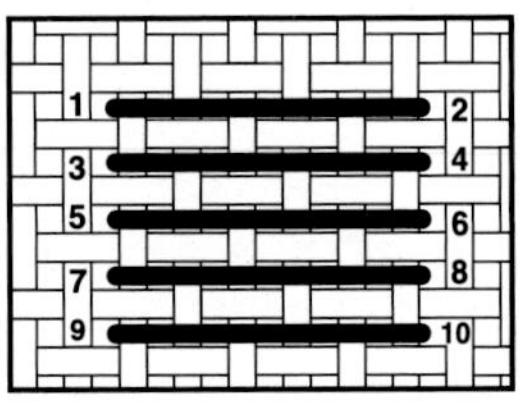

Stem Stitch: This continuous stitch is worked from left to right. Come up at 1 and go down at 2. Holding the floss below the row of stitching, come up at 3 and go down at 4 (**Fig. 16**). Continue working in the same manner to the end of row.

Fig. 16

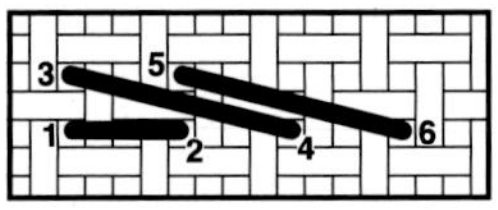

STITCHING TIP

Working over Two Fabric Threads: When working over two fabric threads, the stitches should be placed so that vertical fabric threads support each stitch. Make sure that the first Cross Stitch is placed on the fabric with stitch 1-2 beginning and ending where a vertical fabric thread crosses over a horizontal fabric thread (**Fig. 17**).

Fig. 17

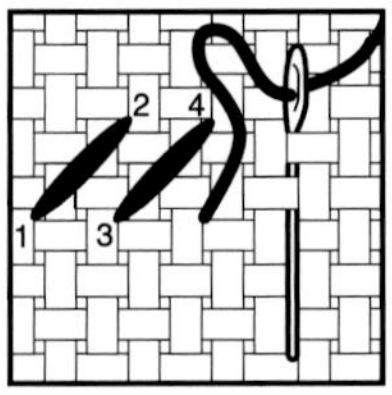

BLESS OUR HOME PILLOW FINISHING

Project shown on page 5.

Trim stitched piece to measure $4\frac{3}{4}$" x $5\frac{1}{4}$". Cut a piece of fabric the same size as stitched piece for backing. For cording, cut one 2" x 28" bias fabric strip and a 28" length of 12" diameter purchased cord. For hanger, you will need a 12" length of $\frac{3}{8}$"w ribbon, and two $\frac{3}{8}$" buttons.

For cording, center cord on wrong side of bias fabric strip; matching long edges, fold strip over cord. Using zipper foot, baste along length of strip close to cord; trim seam allowance to $\frac{1}{2}$". Matching raw edges and beginning at bottom edge, pin cording to right side of stitched piece, making a $\frac{3}{8}$" clip in seam allowance of cording at each corner. Ends of cording should overlap approximately 2"; pin overlapping end out of the way. Starting 2" from beginning end of cording and ending 4" from overlapping end, sew cording to stitched piece. On overlapping end of cording, remove $2\frac{1}{2}$" of basting; fold end of fabric back and trim cord so it meets beginning end of cord. Fold end of fabric under $\frac{1}{2}$"; wrap fabric over beginning end of cording. Finish basting cording to stitched piece. Trim seam allowances diagonally at corners; turn pillow right side out carefully pushing corners outward. Stuff pillow with polyester fiberfill and blind stitch opening closed.

For hanger, (referring to photo) turn one end of ribbon $\frac{3}{4}$" to the back; position on pillow placing button on ribbon. Sewing through ribbon, attach button to pillow. Repeat with opposite end of ribbon and remaining button.

Embroidery floss provided courtesy of The DMC Corporation.

Production Team: Writer – Carolyn Breeding; Editorial – Kimberly L. Ross; Lead Graphic Artist – Chaska Richardson Lucas; Graphic Artists – Karen F. Allbright and Shalana D. Frisby; and Photo Stylist – Karen Hall.

Made in U.S.A.